Elsie Spathari
Ephor of Antiquities

NAUPLION - PALAMIDI

A guide to the history and archaeology

HESPEROS EDITIONS
Athens 2000

ISBN 960-8103-11-8

Elsie Spathari
Ephor of Antiquities

NAUPLION - PALAMIDI

A guide to the history and archaeology

Publisher:
NIKOS KRITSELAS
Translation:
ALEXANDRA DOUMAS
Textual editor:
DEMETRA K. KRITSELA
Layout:
CHRYSSI DASKALOPOULOU
Photographs:
CHR. DASKALOPOULOU - I. PATRIKIANOS
Typesetting - Electronic Pagination:
M. & S. SPILIOU OE
Colour Separation, electronic montage:
COLOUR PLUS
Printed by:
ATH. PETROULAKIS ABEE

Nauplion

Nauplion, set in a magnificent natural landscape, in the shadow of a low rocky peninsula and a high steep hill on the innermost east side of the Argolic Gulf, seems to rise out of the surrounding sea.

Located at the southern end of a route linking major centres where Hellenic civilization flourished at various times - Mycenae, Argos, Tiryns and Nauplion - it has been a focus of culture for thousands of years and still dazzles man with its brilliant past.

Over time Nauplion has attracted and assimilated cultural elements of diverse provenance. By the same token, foreigners have been enchanted by the magic of this privileged place and thrilled by its spectacle. All too often Nauplion has paid a heavy price for this charm. Its history is checkered with violence and destruction, bloody conflicts, massacres and pillage.

Incursion and conquest have dominated its course for millennia and every invader, every ruler has left his mark. These are imprinted on the town's aspect even today, for Nauplion is a creation of the cultures that have passed through it, each leaving something behind.

The amalgam of successive eras, the mixture of ancient, Renaissance and Baroque, the simultaneous presence of Neoclassicism and Eclecticism, all teach a lesson of harmony in which *nobility* triumphs.

Everything is at once old and new, dead and alive. The past is present everywhere and the present is founded deep in the past, always in absolute concord.

In this town modern man, sensitive man, encounters a miracle of different signs of different ages, that mingle and merge in an atmosphere of spell-binding serenity.

MYTH AND HISTORY

In earliest times the Argolid was the cradle of great cultures and the hearth of the most ancient and significant Greek myths. Later, in historical times, these were the nucleus of the Epics and dramatic poetry, originally inspiring the literature and the visual arts of the ancient Greeks, and subsequently influencing Western Civilization.

The myths of the Argolid contain a wealth of information on local traditions concerning the founding of various settlements and the emergence of important prehistoric centres. They lead through the eponymous heroes, and mainly the birth of the first man, Phoroneus, as well as the existence of one of the two great 'inventors' in Greek mythology, Palamedes, towards the interpretation of the Prehellenic past and of Greek prehistory in general.

These myths crystallize memories of local dynastic rivalries, of settlement, of religious and primarily political relations not only between the Argolic cities themselves but also between them and other cities and peoples in the Hellenic world. They are, moreover, associated with the mixing and movement of populations in the region or migrations to lands near and far.

These local myths and the genealogy of the gods, demi-gods and eponymous heroes of the Argolid, demonstrate the close connections of all the region's settlements with Argos. Argos was in essence the centre, the source of the entire mythical world, the aetiology of both the fanciful subjects and the historical memories contained in these myths.

Myths of ancient Nauplia

(modern Nauplion)

The myths referring to the distant past of the ancient city of Nauplia are linked with water, rain, springs, vegetation, the religious rites of Lerna, 'arid and parched Argos', as well as with the open sea, the long and dangerous voyages of mariners and their encounters with sea daemons.

Founder (oikistes) and eponymous hero of Nauplia was Nauplios, son of the sea god Poseidon and the maiden of the springs Amymone, daughter of Danaos.

Tradition has it that when Danaos, ancestor of the Argeians, came from Egypt to Argos with his fifty daughters, the whole region was 'waterless'. The drought was caused by Poseidon, who was angry because the Inachos river, founder of the city, had voted in favour of Hera or Athena in her contest with the god of the sea. Danaos sent his daughters to find water. Amymone discovered a spring, but as soon as she approached to draw water from it, the spring disappeared into the earth.

The tale of Amymone and the spring is told by many ancient authors in various versions.

According to Apollodoros (II, 1,4-5), Danaos's beautiful daughter set off on her father's orders to find water from a spring. In the course of her search she aimed an arrow at a deer, but this accidentally struck a sleeping satyr instead.

1. Poseidon, Amymone and the winged Eros. Representation from an Attic red-figure hydria *of the 4th c. BC. Athens, National Archaeological Museum, inv. no. 12546.*

2. Representation of Poseidon and Amymone from an Attic red-figure hydria *by the Aegisthus Painter, 470 BC. Athens, National Archaeological Museum, inv. no. 1174a.*

1

2

The satyr tried to ravish Amymone, but Poseidon appeared and her frightened attacker fled. The grateful maiden then agreed to lie with the god who led her to find water and showed her the Lerna spring.

According to other writers, as Poseidon threw his trident in pursuit of the satyr, it struck a rock and rent it deeply. From the cleft burbled a spring, which was named after Amymone.

Both versions of the myth relate that fruit of the union of Poseidon and Amymone was Nauplios.

The ancient Greeks represented this myth of Poseidon and Amymone in a host of works during the Early Classical period. This is probably due to its revival in Aeschylus's satirical play *Amymone*.

Nauplios was born in Euboea, whence his mother was carried by the waves after she had lain with Poseidon. As a young man he took part in the Voyage of the Argonauts. He became a brave seafarer and an excellent astronomer, discovering the constellation of Ursa Minor. He set sail from Euboea with his ships and voyaged to the Argolic Gulf, dropping anchor at 'Apobathros', in front of the rocky peninsula, where he built the city of Nauplia.

Nauplios must have lived to a ripe old age, since he continued his activity after the Trojan War. His role in Panhellenic events over many years gave rise to the belief that there were two men named Nauplios, one the son of Poseidon and the other his descendant, several generations later, who was considered to be the founder of ancient Nauplia.

However, the activity of the first Nauplios in much earlier periods does not necessarily mean that there was a second, younger, Nauplios who lived at the time of the Trojan War. There are numerous heroes in Greek mythology whose deeds span many years and who participated in almost all the Panhellenic events, since this enhanced their valour and prestige.

Nauplios married Klymene, daughter of Katreus son of Minos, and sired three sons, Palamedes, Oiax and Nausimedon. All took part in the Trojan War, where Palamedes distinguished himself by his braveness and wisdom. He was honoured by Ajax and Achilles as their equal, but envied by Odysseus because he was cleverer than him and not deceived by his trickery. Odysseus hatched a fiendish plot and accused Palamedes of collaboration with the enemy camp. The Greeks believed Odysseus and condemned Palamedes to death by stoning. When Nauplios heard of this he avenged the besiegers of Troy, first inciting many of the wives of the leaders to commit adultery and then dashing their ships against the rocks at Kaphyreus (modern Cavo d'Oro), by lighting decoying bonfires. He himself is said to have had a similar end.

The way in which Nauplios took revenge on the victors-heroes of the Trojan War belies his close relationship with his father Poseidon, his identification with an evil sea daemon and his connection with Euboea as his birthplace.

Nauplios's revenge was dramatized by the ancient tragic poets Sophocles, Philokles, Astydamas, Lykophron and Timotheos, who wrote a dithyramb entitled *Nauplios*.

However, in myth the founder of Nauplia is presented as a sagacious seafarer and not as an evil sea daemon. This shows that the myth evolved over time, passing from Euboea to the Argolid.

Nauplios bequeathed his knowledge of astronomy and navigation routes to mankind through his son Palamedes, who became Nauplia's most illustrious hero and was, together with Prometheus, the inventor *par excellence* in Greek mythology. His name Palamedes, which is now borne by the lofty crag that looms protectively over the city of Nauplion (Palamidi), expresses the man who thinks and creates with his hands (originally Palamomedes: Greek palame = palm), even though the inventions attributed to him are more revealing of his intellectual skills. He taught men the tactics of warfare and the rules of social life, writing, the alphabet (he added letters to the Phoenician one), the numbers, the use of coinage, weights and measures. He invented the division of time, the sequence of the meals, the mixing of wine with water, *phryktories* (a kind of semaphore), even dice as a pastime for the heroes in the hours of relaxation. A physician as well as an astronomer, he was above all a prudent ancestor for the ancient Greeks who loved and perfected the arts.

Later sources locate Palamedes's tomb on Lesbos, where there was a sanctuary dedicated to him and a statue. The place name 'Palamedeion' is also known in Asia Minor.

Of the ancient works mentioning the myth of Palamedes we cite here the tragedies *Palamedes* by Aeschylus, *Odysseus Enraged* and *Palamedes* by Sophocles, and *Palamedes* by Euripides, all of which have been lost. However, two early Sophist texts (*gymnasmata*), *Palamedes* by Gorgias which is an apologia of the hero himself, as well as *Odysseus. Against Palamedes's treachery*, by Alkidamas, have survived.

Palamedes is rarely represented in ancient art. There is however an early figure of him painted on a clay die of the seventh century BC (Athens, National Archaeological Museum).

Endowed by their great benefactor and ancestor, the Nauplians proved themselves inventive not only in seafaring but also in agriculture. Local tradition attributes to them the pruning of vines, which they proceeded to practice after observing that vines whose branches had been nibbled by a donkey yielded more grapes. This is why there was a stone-carving with a representation of an ass in the ancient city.

HISTORY

Antiquity

There is very little information on ancient Nauplia and its citizens. What is known we owe mainly to the geographer Strabo (VIII, 368-9) and the traveller Pausanias (II, 38, 2-3). There is also a rare reference to Nauplia in the Classical period, in Euripides's play *Orestes*: its harbour is mentioned as the place where Menelaos disembarked on his return from Troy, in order to go to Argos (lines 53-56).

The archaeological finds from the ancient city are limited too. Nevertheless, it is certain that the site was inhabited from at least the Neolithic Age.

Nauplia, with its sheltered harbour, must have been the outport of prehistoric Tiryns, while on the Acronauplia, the rocky peninsula on which defensive walls were raised by all the cultures that succeeded its first fortification, there are scant traces of this first habitation. A small section of the Cyclopean wall of the Mycenaean period still exists near the south corner of the Castello di Toro, indicating the existence of a fortified Mycenaean citadel.

The discovery of a large cemetery on the lower north slope of precipitous Palamidi, in the neighbourhoods of Evangelistria and Pronoia, a little further away, attests the existence of a corresponding settlement in the Early Helladic and the Mycenaean period. The poor finds from the rock-cut graves show that 'some lineages of humble nobles, without power and influence, perhaps subject to the rulers of Tiryns, were buried there in the rocks of Palamidi, in the 12th c. BC, when the Mycenaean civilization was on the wane...' as Semni Karouzou remarked in her book on Nauplion. Burials dating from early historical times, found in the same cemetery, indicate the continuity of life in the same place. In those years Nauplia developed into a powerful city and a rival to Argos.

The presence of Nauplia in the Amphictyony of Kalaureia and indeed the information that it was one of its seven founding cities, shows its importance during the 8th century BC. The meteoric rise of Argos under Pheidon's power and its expansionist ambitions led the remaining cities (Prasies, Nauplia, Arcadian Orchomenos, Athens, Aegina, Epidauros, Hermione) to institute a rival amphictyony as a reaction to the domineering Argeian state.

The development of Nauplia was cut short in the 7th century BC by the dominant power of Argos, when its king, Damokratidas, destroyed it in 600 BC because it was an ally of Sparta. The Spartans allowed those citizens who survived to settle in Methone, Messenia. Argos took Nauplia's place in the amphictyony and the coastal city was henceforth used as a naval base and port by the Argeians.

In the Hellenistic period Nauplia was once again a notable centre, as was neighbouring Asine. Around 300 BC the westernmost and highest part of the Acronauplia was fortified with a polygonal wall, sections of which still survive, incorporated in the later fortifications.

A few remains of Hellenistic houses have been found on the site of the Acronauplia, which together with the strong city walls point to the continuing importance of Nauplia for the security and defence of the region.

The only mention of Nauplia in subsequent years is in the battle before Argos, with Agesilaos, King of Sparta, when 'Cretans having sped to Nauplia' saved the allies who had been trapped outside its walls during the encampment of Pyrrhos.

Several centuries elapsed between Strabo's visit and his reference to the ancient city as 'naval base' of the Argeians, and Pausanias's arrival in Nauplia. Nevertheless the latter traveller beheld the walls, now ruined, and the sanctuary of Poseidon on the Acronauplia (its name is literary and contemporary). It was only to be expected that in the city founded by Nauplios, son of Poseidon, the god of the sea was its principal deity. Spolia built into the city's medieval wall perhaps belonged to his temple.

Pausanias also mentions that in Nauplia

3

3. Remains of the Hellenistic fortification at the base of the Venetian tower of the Acronauplia.

there was a spring called 'Kanathos'. The Argeians claimed that Hera bathed in its waters each year and was transformed into a virgin. This mysterious rite was celebrated with occult practices. The source is identified as the still-flowing Aria spring in the Hagia Moni (Holy Monastery) with the church of the Life-bearing Source. Another view is that the spring was located at the foot of Mount Profitis Ilias, very close to Nauplion.

With the appearance of Christianity the ancient gods gradually lost their devotees. Their sanctuaries fell into ruins and during the early centuries of Christendom were gradually covered over by soil, silently awaiting discovery.

THE BYZANTINE AGE AND THE FRANKISH OCCUPATION

The history of the present town of Nauplion goes back at least fourteen centuries. There was apparently a break with the period of Antiquity, particularly since the traveller Pausanias found ancient Nauplia deserted at the time of his visit (2nd c. AD). Nevertheless, there are indications that this place was not abandoned completely.

After the spread of Christianity to the Peloponnese, the Byzantine nobles first decided to send garrisons to the castles of Nauplion and Monemvasia in the 6th century, according to the source. This move was perhaps prompted by the fact that in AD 589, during the Arab incursions, the defenders of Nauplion were the only ones in the whole of Greece who succeeded in expelling the Empire's foes.

It is also known that at that time a settlement, albeit small, existed at the base of the castle in the shadow of the Palamidi.

The ongoing migrations and raids of the Slav tribes, as well as their descent into the Peloponnese, also instigated the shift of populations from the central Peloponnese into its eastern part. So Byzantine Nauplion was created by the refugees whom the invaders forced to settle there.

From the 9th century Nauplion was an organized urban centre, apparently dependent ecclesiastically on Argos since that town's subsequent patron saint, St Peter, is mentioned as Bishop of Argos and Nauplion. This dependency must have continued until the 12th century, since the same title was borne by the founder of the Arian heresy, Leon 'Bishop of Argos and Nauplion', in 1149.

In 963 the famous priest Nikon the 'Repenter' visited Nauplion to preach the word of God. He was given this prosonym (*Metanoite*) when, together with St. Athanasios the Athonite, he tried to bring the Islamicized Cretans back to Christianity and to convert the Saracens, during the reign of Nicephoros Phocas.

Another visitor to Byzantine Nauplion was the Arab geographer Edrisi, who ranked the city among the most notable in the Peloponnese and marks it on his maps as 'Anabolon' (1154), perhaps in relation to Anapli.

The town's strategic position attracted the Byzantines' interest, as the appointment of Nicephoros Karantinos as 'general' of Nauplion, after the crushing defeat of the Arabs in 1032, attests.

In an age when the sea and the coasts

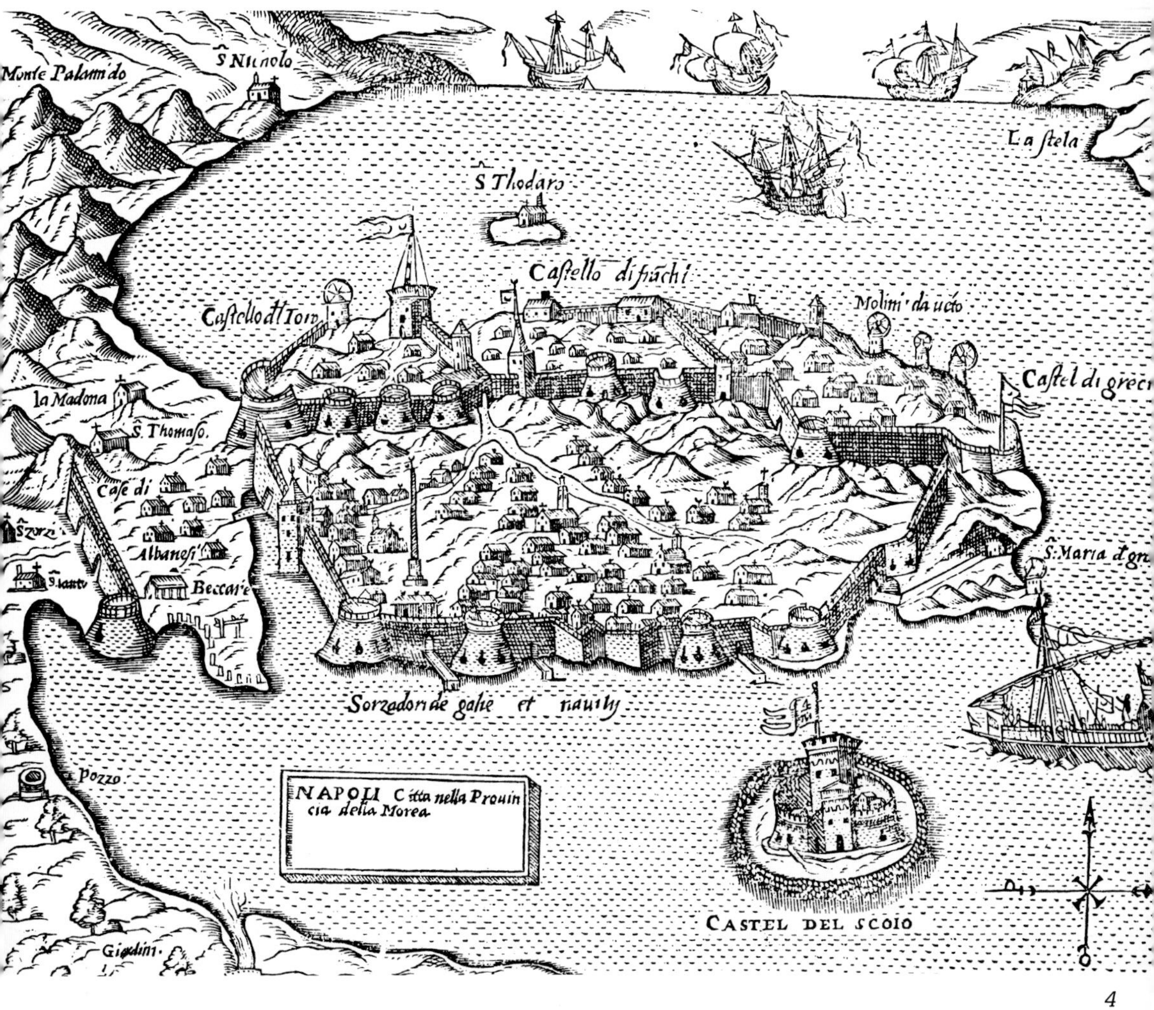

4

4. *Walled Nauplion (Napoli di Romania), as drawn by Comocio (1571).*

were plagued by pirates, the fortified site of Nauplion and its harbour offered safety to its inhabitants. At this time the Acronauplia was fortified and Nauplion developed into an administrative and commercial centre.

In the ensuing years (1180) Emperor Manuel Comnenos appointed a native of Nauplion, (Theodoros?) Sgouros, as overlord of the town. He transformed it into an independent metropolis. In 1199 the emperor charged Sgouros with building a fleet to rid the sea of pirates.

The 12th century was a heyday for Nauplion. The Byzantines fortified the Acronauplia, surrounding it with an enceinte, and this constituted the burg. In many cases the ancient walls were used as foundations for the new ones. The harbour lay to the west, at the tip of the peninsula (today's '*banieres*') while the whole town was protected by walls. There were no houses, walls or doors *extra muros*, only the sea pounding the foot of the protective wall.

In the years just after, pre-eminent figure in Nauplion was Leon Sgouros, son of the previous lord. An able, bold and fearless soldier, he captured the castles of Argos and Corinth in 1203. The following year he laid siege to the castle of Athens, without success, and the castle of Larisa, which he managed to capture. In the meanwhile he had acquired the title of Most August, as son-in-law of Emperor Alexios III Comnenos.

In the year 1204 the Franks, on the pretext of the Fourth Crusade, captured and sacked Constantinople, capital of the Byzantine Empire. They held it until 1261, stripping it of its treasures and paving the way for its final obliteration in 1453.

After the sack of Constantinople Boniface Montferrat, leader of an army of French, Lombards, Flemish and Germans, embarked on the conquest of Greece. The subjugation of the Byzantine provinces to the Crusaders was largely voluntary. The towns passed one after the other into Frankish hands and Boniface marched ahead without armed conflicts. The only resistance put up against the Latins was led by Leon Sgouros, local lord of Nauplion. Boniface laid siege to the city in 1204-1205.

After several successful repulsions, Leon Sgouros fell before the walls of Nauplion and was buried in the narthex of its metropolis (Greek Orthodox cathedral), while his widow surrendered her rights to the Despot of Epirus, Michael Angelos. He sent his brother Theodoros to assume the 'lordship' of Nauplion.

Godfrey Villehardouin, ruler and regulator of matters in the Peloponnese, having taken the Acrocorinth in 1210, besieged Nauplion from land and sea in the same year, with the help of four Venetian ships. After a valiant resistance lasting two years, the starving inhabitants were forced to capitulate and surrendered the castle on the condition that its east section, which was called Castello di Franchi was to be taken by the conqueror, while the Nauplians would keep the west part which has been called Castello di Greci ever since.

The Franks became masters of Nauplion in 1212. Villehardouin immediately ceded his sovereignty to the Burgundian Grand Duke of Athens, Otto de la Roche. Thenceforth until the end of the 14th century, the castles of Anaplion and Argos belonged to the Dukes of Athens, even though they were bequeathed to related families.

In 1308 the de la Roche family bequeathed Nauplion to the related de Brienne family, while in 1356 it was inherited by the d'Enghien family.

In 1377 the last heir of the Dukes, Maria d'Enghien, married the Venetian Pietro Cornaro, who requested the assistance of Venice in 1382. After his death, Maria, foreseeing the imminent dangers from the Accajioli and the despots of Mystras, ceded her rights to the Doge of Venice, Andrea Dandolo, securing for herself and her heirs lifelong allowances. This was how Venice acquired the mightiest castle in the region, which remained in its possession for over 150 years.

VENETIAN RULE

First period of Venetian rule (1389-1540)

In 1389 the Serenissima Republic of Venice acquired the ownership of Nauplion. Having realized for some time that its power balance had been seriously threatened in the Peloponnese, it set its sights on expanding its sovereignty, with the aim of securing suitable strategic points for protecting its trading and naval stations, in order to continue its commercial activities in the East, the source of its wealth. It took two centuries from the Treaty of Sapienza for it to annex Nauplion, a critical site in the Peloponnese, with a safe harbour that met the conditions for establishing itself in the Mediterranean.

Nauplion owes its urban plan to Venice, and mainly in this period.

The first Preditore of Nauplion was Perazzo Malipiero, who was followed by a succession of Venetian *preditori*, *commandatori* and *rettori*, who were either at odds with the Accajioli in Athens or allied with them, as well as with the Byzantines, in order to stem the Ottomans and to prevent their invasion of the Argolid and Corinthia.

In 1396 Yuk-Pasha and Murtaci, on the order of Sultan Vayazit, reached before the walls of Nauplion. The town put up a dynamic resistance, eventually forcing Vayazit to recall his army.

In 1463 Mohamet II the Besieger sent the Pasha of Athens to attack Nauplion. He first defeated the Venetians just before the Isthmus of Corinth. Concurrently, the vizier Mahmut-Pasha arrived outside Nauplion with an army of 80.000 men.

A battle took place in which 5.000 Ottomans were killed but without managing to capture the strongly fortified town, with walls designed by master military engineers from Venice.

After the fall of the castles in Messenia, Vayazit II attacked Nauplion repeatedly, but never captured it. With the treaty of 1502, however, although the town remained with the Venetians it was in the eye of the Ottoman storm.

In 1537 Sultan Suleiman I entrusted the conquest of the legendary town to his vizier Kasim-Pasha. It was then that the hill of Palamidi was used for the first time by the besiegers. Kasim installed his heavy artillery there. The Acronauplia and the lower city were destroyed by the constant bombardments and there were great numbers of casualties. In the end, after a three-year siege, Venice was obliged to sign a peace treaty and the garrison commander of Nauplion, Alexander Kontaris, handed over the keys of the city to Kasim-Pasha. In 1540 the Turks entered Nauplion, while the Venetians and many Greeks left by ship for Venice, the Ionian Islands and Crete.

The new town

The first period of Venetian rule, which lasted 150 years, was in essence the period when the town was created. Till then the Nauplians lived inside the fortified Acronauplia, perhaps because of fear of pirates, and the waves lapped the bottom of the cliff. The presence of the great power of the Serenissima Republic and the systematic fortification of the Acronauplia, according to the latest specifications for protecting a town, gave the impetus for expansion to the northern foothills of the rocky promontory facing the Argolic Gulf. The 'opening' of the town *extra muros* took place around 1500.

Immediately after their installation, the Venetians reinforced the existing fortifications of the Franks and Greeks on the Acronauplia and then extended the fortification eastwards by adding the Castello di Toro (the Latin word *torus* means height).

In order to complete the fortification and protection of the harbour, they erected a small castle on the small islet or reef at its entrance. Originally called Scoglio di S. Theodoro, it was known later as 'Castello' or 'Burdzi' (a Turkish word meaning 'fortification in the sea').

The Venetians paid particular care to the city's harbour. They created an inner harbour by constructing a small breakwater from the land towards Burdzi, for the loading and unloading of small vessels. They also narrowed the passage into the harbour, by arranging the seabed accordingly, in order to control the entry and exit of ships. Burdzi is said to have been linked to the mainland by a chain which was placed there at night, which is why it is also known as the Porto Catena harbour (Italian *catena* = chain).

Preditore Bartholomew Minio took the major decision to expand the city outside the walls, into the marshy area to the north. This was necessitated by the fact that a large population had gathered in Nauplion, mainly of refugees from areas of the Peloponnese that the Venetians had lost to the Ottomans.

The city's infrastructure was laid out by specialist engineers brought from Venice. So the Venetians created a new city modelled on their own. The fill was made with foundations on wooden piles. The roads were opened in a rectangular grid with two basic thoroughfares: from north to south linking the Sea Gate with the Castello di Toro, and from west to east linking the Land Gate with the Foro or central square. The new city was protected by a circuit wall and supplied with water from the Areia springs brought along a built aqueduct.

Nauplion grew into one of the loveliest, wealthiest and most populous cities in the East. Census figures for 1530 give a population of some 10.000 souls.

First period of Ottoman rule (1540-1686)

During the 150 years or so of the first period of Ottomam rule Nauplion became capital of the sanjak of the Morea and seat of its General Commander, the Mora-Valeshi. The Ottomans granted Nauplion many privileges, which fact showed that they considered it the most important town in the Peloponnese.

Despite the damaged buildings and depleted population as a result of the protracted siege, Nauplion soon revived and was enhanced as an important centre of export and import trade for the entire Peloponnese. Its rapid development led many of those who had left after the capitulation to return home.

Greeks formed the greater part of the population, living harmoniously alongside the Ottomans and very few Jews. However, for all the peaceful coexistence, in 1655 the Neomartyr Anastasios of Nauplion was brutally killed by the Ottomans for refusing to convert to Islam. Anastasios became patron saint of Nauplion and his feast is celebrated on 1 February.

In 1686 Nauplion had 8.000 citizens and 3.000 Ottoman soldiers. The town enjoyed an economic and intellectual floruit. Even though there are no architectural remains from this period, we know from the texts that the ruined houses were rebuilt and the town as well as the Acronauplia, known as Its Kale by the Ottomans (a Turkish word meaning inner fortress), filled with large public or private buildings: mosques, fountains and hamams (bath-houses). The headquarters of the Mora-Pasha dominated the central square.

As the 17th century dawned Venice had lost much of its former glory. The gradual loss of its possessions in the Mediterranean, as well as a series of unsuccessful military campaigns in Dalmatia obliged the Venetians to return to the idea of winning back the Greek territories, particular in the Peloponnese. It took action immediately after the fall of Crete to the Ottomans in 1669.

The Venetian general Francesco Morosini had direct knowledge of the strategic and commercial value of Nauplion and decided to concentrate on regaining it. His expedition was organized with great speed and in 1686 he laid siege to the town from land and sea. Constant cannon-fire destroyed its fabric completely; twenty-two churches were demolished and only thirty houses remained standing. The entire southeast quarter was deserted when the powder store located close to the Land Gate was blown up and the aqueduct that passed this way was destroyed.

The continuous offensives of the Venetians forced the Ottomans to sue for peace, surrender Nauplion and withdraw on honourable terms. Morosini entered the city in triumph and received the demands of the Greek Community to keep its privileges of autonomy.

The whole operation impressed Ottomans and Venetians alike. A few months later, while he was still in Greece, Morosini was elected Doge of Venice.

During the first period of Ottoman rule the first foreign travellers reached the city of Nauplion, in the late 16th century. Their descriptions, plans and drawings give us our only picture of it, since nothing now remains of its Oriental ambience. Among the travellers was Evliya Çelebi, an Ottoman who came to Nauplion in the 17th century and describes the way of life, the houses and the mosques of his fellow Muslims there.

Sole surviving monument of this period is the small mosque on the east side of what is now Syntagma Square, the old Venetian Foro, also known as the Square of the Plane Tree of the Struggle. It is nowadays called the 'Trianon'.

Second period of Venetian rule (1686-1715)

Although the second period of Venetian rule lasted only twenty-eight years is was particularly significant for Nauplion. It is hard to believe that in such a short interval such important and large-scale works were achieved. When, after almost 150 years, the Venetians returned to Nauplion they realized, on seeing the fortifications that they themselves had erected and which had remained virtually unharmed, that these were inadequate for the needs of the age.

Times had changed.

They had to make Nauplion an impregnable fortress if they wanted to keep their foothold in this region.

Continuous pressures exerted by the Ottoman foe as well as the every tightening noose around them forced the Venetians to act without delay.

They first laid out the entire area of the Acronauplia, reinforcing its eastward defences, repairing the walls, strengthening the enceinte of the lower city by constructing the east wall and above all erecting a fortress on Palamidi, a project which was a model of the military engineering in that period.

Nauplion was declared capital of the Kingdom of the Morea, seat of the Proveditore Generale and general-in-chief of the East. It was also capital of the province of Romania, hence its name, 'Napoli di Romania'. The population, which had declined as a result of the wars and sieges, was increased by resettling Greek families from the Ottoman-held parts of the Peloponnese and from Athens. By 1700 the town had 5.904 inhabitants.

Before Morisini departed to take up office as Doge, he repulsed a new Ottoman raid in 1687. After his departure there were three Proveditori Generali, until Venice once again entrusted him with the supreme command. Morosini returned to Nauplion in 1693, to hold back again the Serasker of the Peloponnese and to capture Chalkis. He died suddenly on 14 May 1694, in his dear Napoli di Romania. After his death there was terrible strife between Venetians and Ottomans, until the Peace of Karlowitz in 1699, which permitted the Venetians to continue fortifying Nauplion.

According to the testimonies of contemporary preditori and the chroniclers, during the final phase of this second period of Venetian rule, Nauplion was transformed into 'a European city in every way'. It was the most famous, the most noble, the most admired and the 'most beautiful of the cities in the East, the pre-eminent fortress of the flourishing kingdom of the Morea'. It was then that churches and public buildings were put up, some of which still grace the modern town.

In 1713 the Arsenal was built as well as the church of Hagios Nikolaos *extra muros*, and the church of Hagios Spyridon. The church of Hagios Georgios was decorated with frescoes in the Italian style of the 17th century, among them a representation of 'The Last Supper', a copy of the work by Leonardo da Vinci.

However, this heyday was short-lived. In 1714 a new war broke out between Venetians and Turks.

The Preditore of Nauplion, Ieronymo Dolfino left only 1700 men to defend the town when the Serasker Ali Dagut Pasha arrived and encamped outside Tiryns, with an army of 120.000 men, and Çanum Hodja blockaded the harbour of Nauplion with 50 ships. There were epic struggles between the besiegers and the besieged and Nauplion finally fell as a result of the treachery of the French artillery and garrison commander of Palamidi, la Salle. His perfidy was discovered before the fall of the city and the traitor was torn limb from limb, his house pulled down and an anathema put up in its stead, which survived until 1850.

For all the imposing fortification works which made Nauplion the strongest fortress in the world, it was captured after two weeks.

A janizary, the first Ottoman to enter the castle, fixed his yatagan above the gate in the east wall. Tradition has it that every Friday, the day the city was taken, it dripped blood.

Second period of Ottoman Rule (1715-1822)

Straight after the fall of Nauplion it was visited by Sultan Ahmet III, who expressed his gratitude to the victors and granted them privileges. The town was once again designated capital of the Vilayet of the Peloponnese. However, in 1786 the Mora-Pasha transferred his headquarters to Tripolis for military reasons.

During this last phase Nauplion began to decline. Stripped of its administrative functions and bereft of most of its Greek

5

5. *View of the town of Nauplion with Palamidi in the background, immediately after liberation from the second period of Ottoman rule. Engraving by K.J. Sterlin, after a drawing by Wolfsenberger, Zurich, Kunsthaus.*

6. View of the town of Nauplion. Watercolour by Jean-Baptiste Hilaire, 19th c.

citizens, who had left for foreign parts, it devolved into a provincial Ottoman town with just a few port and military activities. Relations between Greeks and Ottomans hardened. Most of the townsfolk were Turks who had either returned after the defeat of the Venetians or had been in the victorious army. To the latter the sultan granted privileges and the goods of Greeks who had either abandoned Nauplion or been decimated in the course of its siege. To the former he returned the properties they owned before they had left the town. The few remaining Greeks gravitated to the poor neighbourhood of the Psaromahalas. The population of Nauplion overall was just 4.000.

In aspect Nauplion changed rapidly into an Oriental town, and all reminders of the cosmopolitan, European grandeur it had previously enjoyed were lost.

The town filled with mosques, hamams (turkish bath-houses) and tall, narrow houses with covered balconies (*sahnisia*).

6

In reality it became a 'totally Turkish' town with a filthy harbour and fetid air.

Those foreign travellers who ventured here in the 19th century describe its decadence, the heavy atmosphere due to the suspicious behaviour of the Turks, the curfews and restrictions on circulation in the town. Only the fortifications silently maintained their magnificence, crowning the town's heights.

With the declaration of the War of Independence in 1821, the Greeks set out to capture these castles. Although the first siege of Nauplion from land and its blockade at sea, in April 1821, failed, after a protracted siege the following year the Greeks took Burdzi and Palamidi. On 29 to 30 November 1822, the feast day of St Andrew, D. Moschonisiotis was the first to scale the Achilles bastion, followed by Staikos Staikopoulos who entered the St Andrew bastion. Within three days the Ottomans were forced to hand over the

7

7. The assassination of Ioannis Capodistrias - painting by a folk artist in the church of Hagios Spyridon, Nauplion.

keys of the town to Theodoros Kolokotronis. Nauplion remained free throughout the War of Independence.

Indeed, early in 1823 an edict of the *Bouleutikon* (representative assembly), which was ratified by the *Ektelestikon* (Executive), designated Nauplion as base of the first Greek Government. Four years later, in 1827, the Third National Assembly passed a decree declaring the town as 'Seat of the Government'.

In January 1828 the first President of Greece, Ioannis Capodistrias, disembarked at Nauplion.

NAUPLION FIRST CAPITAL OF GREECE (1828-1834)

The Greeks were fortunate in having as President one of the greatest statesmen of his age. A political personality of international repute, he resigned his post as Foreign Minister of Russia and came to offer his services to his native Greece.

When he landed at Nauplion he had already succeeded in banishing Ibrahim Pasha from the Peloponnese and recapturing Central Greece. In 1830 he gave his fatherland its greatest gift: the London Protocol recognizing the independence of the Greek State.

While in Nauplion Capodistrias struggled on all fronts. It was imperative that the town be rebuilt and its appearance changed. Its population was growing at an alarming rate. He commissioned Stamatis Voulgaris to prepare a town plan and the architect Theodoros Vallianos to implement it. There were many objections, but work began at a rapid pace.

Capodistrias established the first school in Greece applying the Lancastrian or monitorial system of instruction, which was housed in the mosque in Syntagma Square; the 'Central' military academy for officers; the presidential palace; the Tiryns Farm School; the first primary school.

A few years later, on 27 September 1831, Capodistrias was assassinated outside the door of the Hagios Spyridon church and the progress of the fledgeling Greek state was cut short in its infancy.

In February 1832, while Greece was in turmoil, the three guarantor powers, on the initiative of Britain, chose Otto, the second son of King Ludwig of Bavaria, as hereditary monarch of Greece.

One year later the Greeks welcomed him enthusiastically to Nauplion. He remained there for two years until the 'royal throne' was transferred to Athens, which was declared capital of Greece towards the end of 1834. Nauplion remained capital of the Prefecture of the Argolid. It may have lost its contest with Athens then, but it has won the day in preserving its beauty for posterity.

●

8. *Otto landing at the harbour of Nauplion on 6 February 1833. Athens, National Bank of Greece.*

Castles and Fortifications

1. THE ACRONAUPLIA

The long rocky peninsula that thrusts into the sea of the Argolic Gulf, forming the east side of its inner creek, is linked on its east side by a narrow strip of land with the towering hill of Palamidi as well as with the rest of the Argolid. On its lower north slopes spreads the lower town of Nauplion, established there in late 15th century.

Its low eminence (barely 85 m asl) was inhabited continuously from the remote past of this town's prehistory to the present day.

From Antiquity to the late 15th century AD, when the lower town was created, its rocky mass was at once the city and the fortress.

There are very scant remains from Antiquity on Acronauplia and it is uncertain when it acquired its first fortification, the so-called 'Cyclopean walls', as a prehistoric city.

The earliest visible remains are the polygonal walls built on the highest, west part of the Acronauplia in the late 4th or the early 3rd century BC, when a notable settlement developed on this site.

There are sections of Hellenistic walls *in situ* under the later fortifications, which indicate the course of these defences. They began in the southwest, continued along the north flank and closed east forming a cross wall towards the south. The south side was not walled since it is protected naturally by the sheer rock face.

Upon this wall, with its polygonal masonry, the Byzantines founded their fortification in the Early Byzantine period, perhaps extending it to the east.

When the Franks captured the Acronauplia in 1212 it was divided into two castles, the so-called Castello di Greci on the west and highest part, and the Castello di Franchi on the east, which is

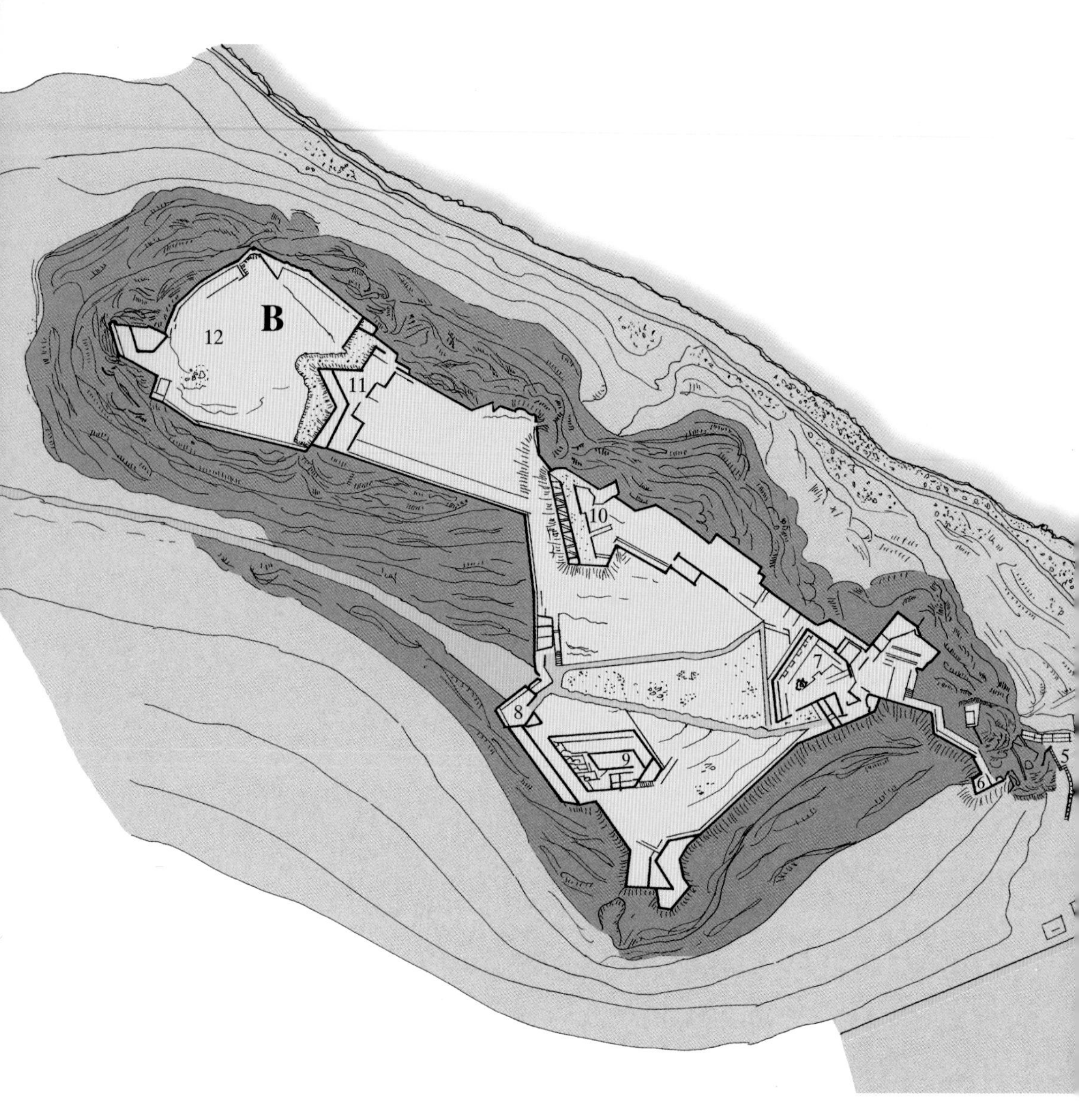

9

divided by an intermediate wall built by the Franks. A tower stands in the middle of the hill, in order to survey the southern town and monitor the access to the Castello di Greci. To the east, the Castello di Franchi is girded by an enceinte with two round towers and a triangular bastion.

There are only a few remnants of the Frankish period and these are restricted to the east side of the Castello di Franchi.

When the Venetians captured Nauplion during the first period of Venetian rule (1389-1540) the walls were in need of repair. In 1470 Preditore Pasqualigo and the engineer Cambello undertook the task of repairing and extending the walls.

Adjacent to the Castello di Franchi, to the east of the fortifications, stands a third

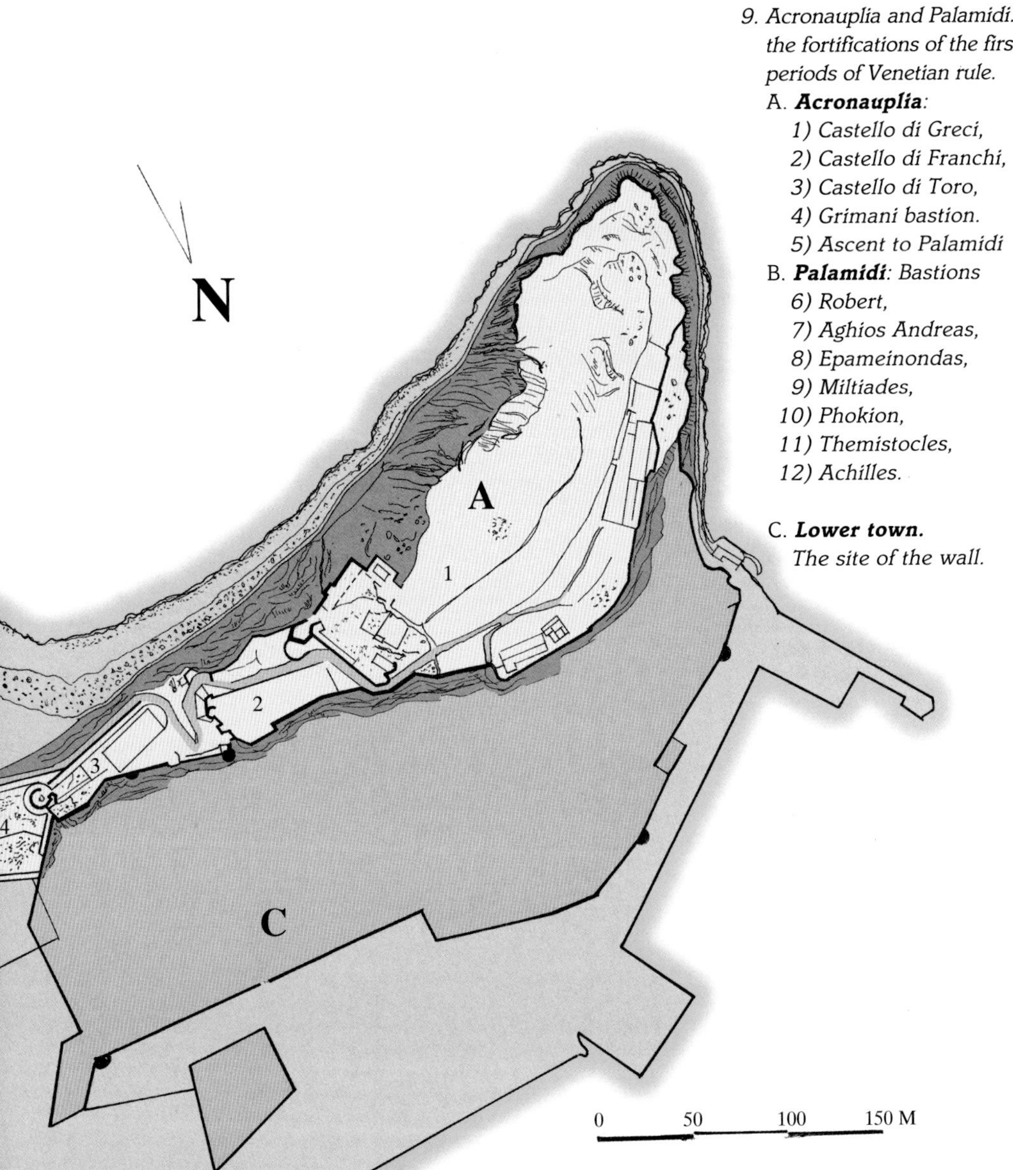

9. *Acronauplia and Palamidi. Plan of the fortifications of the first and second periods of Venetian rule.*
A. ***Acronauplia**:*
1) Castello di Greci,
2) Castello di Franchi,
3) Castello di Toro,
4) Grimani bastion.
5) Ascent to Palamidi
B. ***Palamidi**: Bastions*
6) Robert,
7) Aghios Andreas,
8) Epameinondas,
9) Miltiades,
10) Phokion,
11) Themistocles,
12) Achilles.

C. ***Lower town.***
The site of the wall.

castle, the Castello di Toro. Between the two castles was a wall that ended in a square tower on the seaward side.

On the landward side, at the junction of the two castles, a small tower of truncated conical shape was erected. It still stands today, an outstanding example of military engineering in the late Renaissance. Its gates, vaulted passages, were protected by the high walls with crenellated battlements, achievements of the art of fortification of the age. They still stand *in situ*, as reminders of high-spots in the town's history.

At the east end of the Acronauplia, at the point where it joins to the Argolic plain, a moat (*fossa*) was dug, consistent with the demands of fortress architecture at that time. It was connected to the main gate by a drawbridge.

10

11

10. The Grimani bastion on the east edge of the fortification of the Acronauplia (1706).

11. Acronauplia. The winged lion of St. Mark. Emblem of the Venetians, incorporated in the east bastion, the Grimani bastion.

12. *Acronauplia.*
The famous 'clock'
of Nauplíon.

13. *Acronauplia.*
Part of the
Venetian
fortifications
with battlements.

13

14. Acronauplia. The round tower in the Castello di Toro, with its gate.

Relief lions, incorporated in the walls or below the gates, set their seal on the work, declaring the sovereignty of Venice and the year of their creation.

In 1540 the first period of Venetian rule came to an end, with the advent of the Ottoman Turks who settled in Nauplion for almost a century and a half. Although they renamed the fortress of Acronauplia Its Kale, they made no alterations to the Venetian castles, but merely minimal repairs.

In 1686, when the Venetians returned to Nauplion, they found their castles waiting silent and intact. However, military engineering had changed much in the meantime, in response to the use of cannon. The fortification of Palamidi would make obsolete the defensive importance of Acronauplia. Nevertheless, the Venetians reinforced the walls and towers of the Castello di Toro. They completed the external fortifications at this time, constructing the impressive gate named after Preditore Augustino Sagredo (1713) on

5. *Acronauplia. Detail of the large circular tower of the castle with its crenellated battlements.*

the north side of the Castello di Greci, on the Dolfino bastion.

A small fort was built at the east end of the pensinsula. Named the Grimani bastion by the Proveditore of the Morea, it stands to this day. This bastion protected the Land Gate, which was destroyed but has been restored in recent years.

The castles of Acronauplia can be visited today either from Arvanitia or from the northeast ascent or from the terrace on which the Xenia Hotel stands.

However, the finest view is without doubt from the top of Palamidi, from where one can see and understand the arrangement of the castles on the Acronauplia: at the westernmost and highest edge the Castello di Greci, in the middle the Castello di Franchi and in the lowest, easternmost part the Castello di Toro abutting the Grimani bastion.

16

16. *Palamidi. The west inside face of the crag, with the stepped ascent and the Robert bastion.*

17. Palamidi. The Phokion bastion. 17

2. PALAMIDI

The most important fortification project for the protection of Nauplion was implemented in the second period of Venetian rule (1686-1715) on the summit of the massive stone crag of Palamidi that overshadows the east side of the town.

This remarkable work, meeting fully the requirements of the art of fortification in the age of large cannon and artillery guns, is due originally to the Venetian general Morosini. It was he who utilized this rocky hill during the siege of Nauplion in 1686 and who conceived the idea of constructing such a fortress complex on its highest peak (216 m asl).

As soon as the Venetians conquered Nauplion they assessed the value of its position for safeguarding the Serenissima's sovereignty as mistress of the seas and set about transforming it into an impregnable fortress, the most strongly fortified of those then existing in Greece. Work began straight after the Treaty of Karlowitz in 1699, with the construction of new fortifications on the Acronauplia and in the lower city, as well as on precipitous Palamidi, for the first time.

When the first Proveditore of the Morea, Jacobo Corner, left his post in 1690 he wrote to the Venetian Senate that he had the providence to capture and to fortify the summit of Palamidi which, as it dominates the city, threatened it 'terribly'.

Throughout the second period of Venetian rule the hitherto unfortified and uninhabited Palamidi was surrounded by a wall, erected with remarkable speed and care, and completed with particular zeal.

The ingenious design of the fortress complex was devised by the Dalmatian Giaxich and the French engineer la Salle, who together with his fellow countryman Levasseur supervised the construction of the work as well (1711-1714). It is incredible that such a large project was completed within such a short time. Large numbers of soldiers and labourers were employed for its construction, so that during the new raid by the Ottomans the Commandatore of the Venetians, Augustino Sagredo, and the Proveditore Generale, Ieronymo Dolfino, sped to advise Venice that the necessary works had been carried out for the fortification of Nauplion, which was now inviolable.

A fortress of such wondrous size and majesty, yet so in keeping with the natural landscape and the huge, steep hill, is a rare creation indeed.

The Palamidi castle consists of eight independent bastions developed in stepped arrangement around a central west-east axis crossing the crest of the hill. Placed at different levels of unequal height, they are positioned in such a relationship to each other that each is independent yet there is the possibility of mutual support, or even the possibility of attacking them. All are protected outside by a mighty rampart, in which they are sometimes incorporated and which sometimes follows its own circuit, reinforced by strong towers. In the large bastions there was accommodation for the soldiers, provision for storing ammunition and food, and cisterns for collecting rainwater. Most were equipped with bronze cannon of the very latest technology, that were brought from the renowned factory of I. Francisco Alberghetti in Venice, while on the battlements of all there were loopholes for numerous defenders.

The bastions were named originally after the Venetian proveditori, whose coats of arms were built into the façades of their gates. So the names Morosini, Sagredo, Dolfino and Grimani are encountered. Later, when the Ottomans captured the castle and town, the bastions were given Turkish names, and last, when the Greeks took Palamidi, they gave them ancient Greek names or saints' names, by which they are still known today.

There are two ascents to Palamidi. On foot from its west side, where there is the famous staircase, and by vehicle from the tarmac road that leads as far as the east gate of the castle.

On the west side of the hill, towards the town, a stairway of 857 steps led up to the fortress. At the bottom of the hill it was associated with the Grimani bastion. Initially lower, it was roofed by vaults at intervals, so that it was illuminated by

18. Palamidi. The interior of the Aghios Andreas bastion with the chapel dedicated to St Andrew.

sunlight, and reinforced with battlements for its defence. Higher up it was free, because it could not be breached at such a height and was concurrently defended by the castle.

The first fortification the visitor encounters as he/she climbs up the stairway to Palamidi is the small Robert bastion (Deniz-tapia in Turkish) which is half way up towards the west peak of the hill. It was named after the heroic French colonel who fell during the siege of the Acropolis at Athens.

When the visitor reaches the top he/she faces the first large bastion, of St Andrew (Aghios Andreas). This was originally named after Proveditore Augustino Sagredo, as recorded in the inscription preserved on the plaque with the relief winged lion of Venice, built in the wall above the great gateway of the bastion. According to the Latin inscription this bastion, built in 1712, housed the Garrison Commandery, for which reason it was called Jidar-tapia during the second period of Ottoman rule, because the headquarters of the commander were housed

19. Palamidi. The Miltiades bastion, which is the largest bastion and independent from the other seven.

here. There were also specially arranged quarters for billetting the soldiers. Its interior housed at first the small church of St Augustine and later the present chapel of Hagios Andreas o Protokletos (St Andrew the First-called). The visitor climbs a large step to reach the top of the bastion, from where there is a superb vista of the town of Nauplion and the Argolic Gulf.

As the visitor leaves the St Andrew bastion, to the north is the Leonidas bastion, which the Ottomans called Tobrak-tapia. It is trapezoidal in plan and its walls stand to a considerable height. From here there is a view of the neighbourhood of Pronoia below and the road leading to Tiryns and Argos beyond.

The Miltiades bastion (the Ottomans' Bazirian-tapia), the largest and most freestanding of the eight bastions, rises northeast of the preceding one. It is an independent fort of quadrilateral plan, with

20. *Palamidi. The passage towards the Aghios Andreas bastion.*

21

21. *Palamidi.*
Aerial photograph
of the castle
and its bastions.

22

22. The entrance to the Aghios Andreas bastion, with the lion of St Mark incorporated in the wall.

walls 22 m high. On top of it are several gun emplacements and loopholes from which the defenders were able to fire at all the surrounding fortifications as well as at what lay lower down. It has a huge cistern for rainwater and seven vaulted-roofed cells were criminals sentenced to death were jailed and executed in quite recent times (1840-1920).

The chief general of the Greeks in the War of Independence, Theodoros Koloko-

23

23. Palamidi. The dungeon in which Kolokotronis was imprisoned, in the Miltiades bastion.

24. Palamidi. Part of the Miltiades bastion with the tunnels that became cells of prisoners sentenced for life (1840- 1920).

tronis, was imprisoned in the Miltiades bastion along with his chief captain, Plapoutas, by the regents of King Otto, who was still a minor. The heroes were charged with high treason and sentenced to death, because the 'Old Man of the Morea', as Kolokotronis was known, had been a friend of the great power Russia during the Struggle and was therefore an opponent of the appointed rulers.

At the point where the Miltiades bastion stands, the mighty wall girding the summit of the hill and encircling the bastions curves to the north, forming a triangular terrace. At the northeast corner of this, near the Epameinondas bastion, is the gate where the tarmac road, the second access to the castle, terminates. Over the iron gate closing the Epameinondas bastion there is a plaque carved with the Turkish emblems - a turban, a cudgel and an Arab yatagan - incorporated in the wall. The Ottomans called this bastion Seitan-tapia, i.e. 'devil's bastion'.

Even higher up, on the southeast side of this triangular terrace, stands the Themistocles bastion or Kara-tapia. On its south side, at the foot of the fort, is a steep gorge down to the beach of Arvanitia, so named after the bloody episode of the brutal murder of the Albanian fighters by the Turks, who had called them to help combat the Greeks participating in the Orloff Uprising (1779). The reward for hundreds of fellow Muslim fighters was their death, by being thrown into the void from the Themistocles bastion.

As the visitor follows the course of the wall eastwards, he/she reaches the Achilles bastion, known by the Ottomans as Yurus-tapia because it was from here that they captured Palamidi in 1715. This is closed on its east side by a deep manmade moat (fossa) which also marks the end of the Venetian fortification.

The Achilles bastion, like the Miltiades bastion, was an independent fort. Its wall was not very high, barely 6 metres. From this bastion on the night of 29 November 1822 the leader of the siege of the castle exhorted the freedom-fighters battling for its capture to celebrate the feast of St Andrew 'with the fall of the mightiest fortress of the enemy of Christendom', and ordered an attack. The first to scale it, using a ladder, was Demetrios Moschonisiotis, followed by Staikos Staikopoulos with fifty handpicked men. After the capture of the other bastions, by dawn on 30 November 1822 the Greeks were masters of Palamidi and celebrated mass in the church of Hagios Andreas. Full of joy and emotion they fired while singing 'if all the castles are lost and if all are ruined, may God protect the lovely Palamidi'.

The fall of Palamidi, the 'Gibraltar of Greece' according to de la Gravière, filled the Greek freedom-fighters with courage that lasted throughout the struggle for Independence. This was their symbolic bastion and they defended it with all their forces, so that not even Ibrahim dared to besiege it.

As the visitor continues eastwards beyond the moat, he/she comes to the last bastion, named Phokion, which was built after 1715, during the second period of Ottoman rule. Barracks were constructed on its south side, but these have since been demolished.

3. BOURDZI

The Venetian fortress founded on a rock that rises from the sea at the entrance to the gulf of Nauplion, has stood sentinel of the town's harbour since the first period of Venetian rule. Known as Bourdzi, it is one of Nauplion's most distinctive features, closely linked with its fortunes for hundreds of years.

The islet on which the fortress was built in 1473 was originally called Aghioi Theodoroi, perhaps after a chapel dedicated to the Sts Theodore by Theodoros Angelos, lord of Nauplion before the Frankish Occupation. Called by various names over the centuries - Scoglio di S. Theodoro, Bourdzi, Passage, Castel dal Mar, Thalassopyrgos, Kastelli - the Turkish word Bourdzi, meaning fortress in the sea, eventually prevailed.

In 1470, during the first period of Venetian rule (1389-1540), Preditore Pasqualigo commissioned the architect Antonio Cambello, who had designed the Tori tower on the Acronauplia, to raise a fortress. The project was continued later by the military engineer Brancaleone.

A typical Renaissance construction, it forms part of a single defensive ensemble that includes the other fortresses in the town. It was completed during the second period of Venetian rule, when the tall tower at the centre of the castle was also rebuilt. A chain linked this sea-girt fortress with the harbour on the west side of the Acronauplia, thus closing the entrance to it and controlling the passage of ships in and out.

Bourdzi remained in use as a fortress for the town until the mid-19th century. From 1865 it was the residence of the 'executioners' in the Palamidi prison, while since 1930 it has functioned either as an hotel, a restaurant or a venue for cultural events.

The Town today and its Monuments

Nauplion today, at once a modern and an historical town, keeps in its fabric a large number of monuments covering all periods of its long history.

These monuments, together with the natural landscape, compose its present architectural personality and aspect, since the very old exists alongside the ultra modern, creating a sense of timelessness. The old town spreads along the north side of the low eminence of the Acronauplia, from the col formed between it and the precipitous massif of Palamidi, as far as its western edge that plunges into the sea, while the modern town develops eastwards of it, in the shadow of its famous Kastro (castle).

The boundary between them is marked on the one hand by Capodistrias Square, with its park and statue of Capodistrias, sculpted by M. Tobros, gazing out at the old town, and on the other by the park with the equestrian statue of Kolokotronis, sculpted by L. Sochos, which faces Palamidi. Beside them are the Law Courts, housed in an early 20th century building in the Neoclassical style, in front of which is Dikastirion Square, with the bus station, from where the visitor can begin the tour of the town.

The old town of Nauplion, which begins at the foot of the Acronauplia and descends gradually towards the sea, is founded on natural terraces at different heights and spreads along the entire length of the peninsula, following the natural outline of the hill. The town's three basic road arteries take the same direction, traversing the built-up part from end to end and dividing it into three main sections, corresponding to its urban development at various times.

In order to get to know the town and its monuments, the visitor should set off from its east edge, the arrival point, and follow one of these streets.

27

27. General view of the old town of Nauplion, from Palamidi.

28

29

28. *The recently restored 'Land Gate'.*

29. *The Venetian cannon on the 'Pente Adelphia'*

30. *View of the sea on the north side of the old town of Nauplion, below the walled Acronauplia.*

31. *Palamidi and the town of Nauplion, from Bourdzi.*

30

31

BAKERY
ART
GALLER

32. A street in the old town of Nauplion, as used today.

33. Entrance to the residence of the regent Armansberg.

33

34

35

34. Neoclassical house with bougainvillaeas.

35. Early stone house with bougainvillaeas.

36-37. Stepped streets in the old town.

38. Ottoman fountain with Venetian spolia.

36

37

38

39. *Hagios Georgios. The most historical church in Nauplion (16th century) and the present metropolis (Greek Orthodox cathedral).*

40. *Hagios Spyridon (1702). On 27 September 1831 Ioannis Capodistrias, first President of Greece, was assassinated at the entrance to the church.*

41. *Hagia Sophia. The only Byzantine church in Nauplion, altered by later repairs and additions.*

42. *Metamorphosis tou Soteros. Originally a Catholic monastery, subsequently a mosque and since 1839 the Catholic church, popularly known as the Frangokklesia.*

43. *Panagitsa. A 15th-century church dedicated to the Birth of the Virgin and St Anastasios, patron saint of Nauplion.*

39

40

41

42

43

44

45

44. The Venetian Arsenal. Built in 1713 by Augustino Sagredo, it now houses the Nauplion Archaeological Museum.

45. The 'Bouleutiko'. *A large mosque erected by Aga Pasha in 1730, it was used as the premises of the first Parliament* (boule) *of the Greeks, in 1825.*

46

47

46. The small mosque in Constitution Square (Plateia Syntagmatos). *Built in the first period of Ottoman rule (1540-1686), it is nowadays a venue for cultural events.*

47. Part of the cloisters of the Medrese (Muslim seminary), a building from the second period of Ottoman rule.

48

49

48. Three Admirals Square (Plateia Trion Navarchon).

49. The apothecary shop of Boniface Bonafin, the first pharmacy opened in the town after the Liberation.

50

50. The first grammar school, founded by Otto, is now the Town Hall of Nauplion. A commemorative plaque at its entrance.

51. The Hypsilantis Monument in Three Admirals Square.

51

52

53

52. *The Municipal Art Gallery on the* 'Megalos Dromos'.

53. *The museum of the Peloponnesian Folklore Foundation 'Vasileios Papantoniou'.*

54

55

54. The War Museum is housed in a three-storey Neoclassical building on the site of the first Officer Cadets Academy.

55. The façade of the 'Palamidis' Library.

56

57

56. The church of Hagios Nikolaos on the waterfront.

57. The Nauplion Customs House, designed by Stamatis Kleanthis in the mid-19th century.

58. Philhellenes Square (Plateia Philellinon) *with the monument to the French philhellenes who fell fighting for the cause of Greek independence (1903).*

59. Early Neoclassical and vernacular houses on the sea-front.

58

59

60

61

60. *The Areias Monastery, a Byzantine foundation of the 12th century.*

61. *The 'Bavarian Lion', carved in the rock by the German sculptor Siegel as a heroon to the Bavarians who perished.*

62

62. The pathway in Arvanitia.

63. Karathona bay.

63

The Nauplion Archaeological Museum

The Nauplion Archaeological Museum stands on the west side of Syntagma Square. The impressive building, which houses important finds from the Argolid, from prehistoric times, mainly of the Mycenaean civilization, as well as other periods of Antiquity, is today the most splendid jewel in the town of Nauplion, definitive for its present aspect.

It was built during the second period of Venetian rule (1686-1715) by the Venetian Proveditore Augustino Sagredo and was intended as an arsenal for the fleet - as recorded in the Latin inscription on the marble plaque with the relief lion of Venice, incorporated in the façade.

This stone-built three-storey monument is fronted by a five-arched portico standing on four pillars and upholding the enormous building. Its mass is articulated symmetrically in horizontal and vertical lines and it occupies virtually the entire west side of the square.

The Archaeological Museum is housed in the two upper storeys of the building, while the offices of the IVth Ephorate of Prehistoric and Classical Antiquities are accommodated in the ground floor. The objects are displayed in a long narrow spacious hall on each floor, placed along its axis in cases or free-standing, and in chronological sequence.

Exhibited on the first floor are prehistoric artefacts from various sites in the Argolid. They span all eras, starting from the Palaeolithic Age, followed by objects, vessels and tools of the Mesolithic to 6000 BC from the Caves of Franchthi and Kefalari, and the Neolithic finds (6000-2800 BC) from various sites such as Kefalari, Dendra and Nauplia.

The chronological development continues

◀ *Mycenaean clay female figurine from the Lower Citadel at Tiryns (LH IIIC - 12th c. BC).*

with the Early Helladic objects, such as vases and tools, from Berbati and Tiryns (2800-2000 BC), from where the unique *psychter* of this period comes, the Early Helladic sealings from Asine as well as pottery from Asine, Tiryns and Mycenae. Most of the exhibits in this hall are Mycenaean (1600-1100 BC).

In addition to the finds from the site of Mycenae, the centre of Mycenaean civilization, there are important objects of this period, such as bronze and clay vases from the rich cemetery at Dendra, the citadels at Tiryns and Midea, and Asine.

A host of minor objects, bronze weapons and tools are exhibited in the cases in the prehistoric gallery of the Museum.

A unique find, from the Mycenaean cemetery at Dendra, is a bronze Mycenaean panoply of the 15th century BC. It comprises four pieces: the gorget, the pauldrons, the cuirass and part of the cincture for protecting the body of the warrior.

One of the most important finds of the 13th century BC, from the area of Nauplia, is an *amphora-krater* with pictorial representations on each side, of a chariot drawn by two horses and with two passengers, depicted between stylized palm trees.

A clay, wheelmade figurine of the familiar type of the goddess with raised arms is an important example of Mycenaean coroplastic art. It was found in the small shrine at Tiryns and dates from the 12th century BC. The face, with its prominent nose and very round eyes, and the parts of the body are modelled. The female is bedecked in a diadem, necklaces and bracelets, while her garment is adorned with garlands. The hair, dressed in three long tressess, falls to the thighs. The adjacent figurine of another divine female, a recent find from Midea, rivals the former in beauty. Its tubular body with ample bosom, long neck and proportionately smalll head place it in the group of smaller painted figurines in contradistinction to the larger monochrome figurines, perhaps apotropaic in character, which were found in the cult centre of Mycenae. Elegant with a lively face, on which the eyes are emphasized, and a large *polos* on the head, it dates from the second half of the 13th century BC. Its presence belies the existense of another sacred place on another important citadel in the Argolid, Midea.

Among the numerous Mycenaean figurines is an exhibit unique of its kind, a 13th-century BC figurine from Asine rendering a figure with serious formal expression, popularly known as the 'Prince of Asine'.

There are several Linear B tablets from Tiryns as well as small fragments of wall-paintings from the palace at Tiryns.

Various vases, a stone lamp and bronze weapons are from Nauplia, while *pithamphorae*, a clay lamp, bronze finds, jewellery of amethyst or ivory, sealstones and a gilded bronze cup are from the tholos tomb at Kazarma.

Exhibited in a similar long narrow hall on the second floor of the Museum, again arranged in chronological order, are objects from historical times in the Argolid, as well as some representative pieces from the Corinthia and Boeotia.

Starting from the Submycenaean period, the exhibit spans the entire Geometric period and continues with pieces from the Classical and Hellenistic periods.

Particularly important are the bronze helmet from a Submycenaean tomb at Tiryns, and the Geometric vases and grave goods (1000-700 BC). Unique are the late 8th-century BC terracotta votive shields from Tiryns, decorated with martial and mythological scenes. On one shield, for example, a scene of Achilles with Penthesilea is painted on the inside and depictions of Centaurs with hunters on the outside.

Other important exhibits are the 7th-century BC terracotta ritual masks from Tiryns, with prominent facial features and exaggerated expressions.

The series of figurines of goddesses, enthroned with necklaces and other jewellery or standing holding offerings, comes from the sanctuary of Tiryns. The works are splendid examples of coroplastic art in the Argolid.

The private collections that enrich the Museum include figurines from a Boeotian workshop. The large female bust from the ancient deme of Halieai is also from a Boeotian workshop.

Among the important finds in the Museum are works from the Archaic and Classical periods, such as the Panathenaic *amphora* by the Mastos Painter, with representation of a victor in the horse races (2nd half 6th c. BC), and the red-figure *hydria* with the scene of Orestes murdering Clytemnestra (440 BC).

Depicted on a Boeotian *skyphos* is the episode of Odysseus' stay in the palace of Circe: three of his companions have already been metamorphosed into swine (425-400 BC). A red-figurine *loutrophoros* is decorated with the scene of a wedding procession and a white *lekythos* of the 5th century BC shows two female figures with Hermes *psychopompos* (conductor of souls). A special series of finds includes hydrias of hellenistic times, lamps and alabastra.

Exhibited in the vestibule of the second storey are an Archaic column capital in the Doric order, from Tiryns (7th c. BC), a bust of a philosopher and a bust of a young maiden of the Roman period, as well as a marble grave stele of the Late Classical period, from Nemea.

•

64

65

64. *Jug with cut-away spout* (kymbe), *from Tiryns. 2300 BC.*

65. Psykter, *from Tiryns. Early Bronze Age (2500 BC).*

66-67. *Clay vases, from the Franchthi Cave, Hermionis. Middle Neolithic period (c. 5800-5300 BC).*

66

67

68

68. Mycenaean bronze panoply, from the chamber tomb at Dendra. It comprises four items: gorget, pauldron, the cuirass and successive articulated cinctures that protected the body and are attached to the sheets of the cuirass. 15th c. BC.

69. Bronze helmet, from a tomb at Tiryns. Submycenaean period (late 11th c. BC).

69

70, 71

72

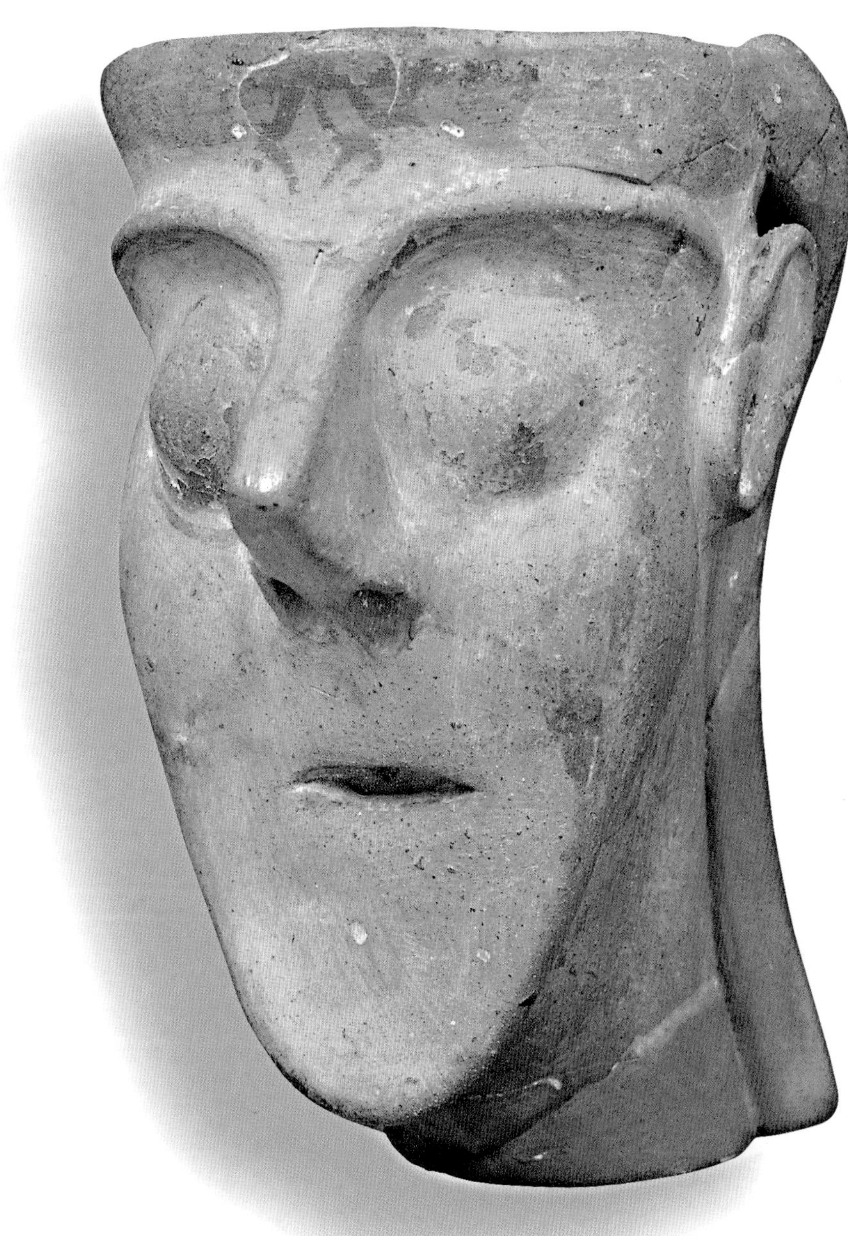

70-71. Clay female figurines from the shrine in the Lower Citadel (R 110) at Tiryns, dated in Late Mycenaean times (LH IIIC, 12th c. BC).

72. Head of a clay figurine, from Asine - the so-called 'Lord of Asine'. LH IIIC (12th c. BC).

73. Stirrup jug from a chamber tomb at Profitis Ilias, Tiryns (2nd half 14th c. BC).

74. Ptotogeometric vases from Asine.

75. Jug with representation of birds, from Asine. Middle Helladic period (1700-1600 BC).

73

74

75

6

76. Pithamphora, *from Pronoia, Nauplion. Late Geometric period (8th c. BC).*

77. Stirrup jug with representation of a chariot, from Evangelistria, Nauplia (13th c. BC).

77

78

79

78. *Terracotta masks, from the* bothros *on the Citadel at Tiryns. 7th c. BC.*

79. *Terracotta figurine of a seated female figure, from the* bothros *on the Citadel at Tiryns. Archaic period.*

80-81. *Terracotta female figurines. Hellenistic period.*

80

81

82-83. Black-figure lekythoi. *Late 6th c. BC.*

84. Red-figure kalyx-krater *with representation of Dionysos and Ariadne. 4th c. BC.*

85. Kalyx-krater *with ivy-leaf band. 4th c. BC.*

82

83

84

85

INDEX
CHRONOLOGICAL PERIODS
Venetian Occupation
Ottoman Occupation
Buildings pre-1828
19th century, 1828-1862
19th century, 1862-1925
20th century, Modern
B
PLATEIA
HAGIOU
NIKOLAOU
KOMNENOU
BLEZI
ARISTEIDOU
MENIATI
FARMAKOPOULOU
GEORGIOU A
SPELIADOU
PLATEIA
SYNTAGMATOS
30 NOEMVRIOU
PSARON
BYRONOS
SPETSON
LABRINIDOU
KONSTANTINOUPOLEOS
ZYGOMALA
ZYGOMALA

OTHONOS
OLGAS
KOTSONOPOULOU
SOFRONI
VAS. ALEXANDROU
YPSILANTOU
SIOKOU
AMALIAS
KOKKINOU
DEMETRIADOU
PLATEIA TRION NAVARHON
TERZAKI
VAS. KONSTANTINOU
PLATEIA
KAPODISTRIOU
VETINI
ANTONOPOULOU
SYNGROU
PLATEIA
NIKITARA
KOKKINOU
DISTRIOU
PLATEIA
HAGIOU
SPYRIDONA
TERTSETI
PLAPOUTA
HAGIOU GEORGIOU
PLATONOS
POTAMIANOU
25 MARTIOU
PAPANIKOLAOU
FOTOMARA
MOUDZOURIDOU
PLATEIA
STAIKOPOULOU
FOTOMARA
0,00
10,00
30,00
50,00
5,00
20,00
40,00

The Nauplion Folklore Museum

The Museum of the Peloponnesian Folklore Foundation 'Vasileios Papantoniou' is housed in the so-called 'Folklore Building', at the junction of Ypsilantou, Sofroni and Vas. Alexandrou streets. Opened in 1974, it boasts rich collections of Greek folk costumes, textiles and weaving tools, handiwork, embroideries and jewellery as well as domestic objects. The Peloponnesian Folklore Foundation, which aimed to create a museum that was simultaneously a high level research centre, quickly emerged as an exemplary and original museum unit. All its exhibits are fully inventoried and photographed, it organizes temporary thematic exhibitions and has a unique library of its kind. In 1989 it set up 'Stathmos', in the engine sheds of the old railway station. This is the venue for its educational programmes and also houses an exhibition of objects associated with the child (furniture, school equipment, toys, theatre etc.). The social, educational and scientific role of the Foundation in the international museum community was rewarded in 1981, when it received the European Museum of the Year Award.

To mark the 25th anniversary of its inauguration, the museum is being completely refurbished and rearranged, in accordance with the latest museological principles.

The Nauplion War Museum

Since 1988 the Nauplion War Museum has been housed in two storeys of the three-storey Neoclassical building at the corner of Amalias and Ang. Terzakis streets.

This was originally the premises of the first Officers' Academy, in 1828-1834, founded by the first president of Greece, Ioannis Capodistrias. The Museum in-/cludes exhibits from all periods of Modern Greek history: engravings of Nauplion, photographs of the heroes of the Greek War of Independence as well as weapons, cannon and sacred heirlooms of various armed struggles. There are photographs and memorabilia from the Macedonian Struggle, the Balkan Wars (1912-1913) and the Asia Minor campaign, as well as of World War II, the Battle of Crete, the German Occupation and the Liberation.

Special emphasis is placed on the contribution of the inhabitants of the Argolid to Greece's struggles for liberation. The Museum has a room for temporary exhibitions.